JOURNAL

PETER PAUPER PRESS, INC.
WHITE PLAINS, NEW YORK

Cover illustration by Lylove Studio

Copyright © 2011
Peter Pauper Press, Inc.
202 Mamaroneck Avenue
White Plains, NY 10601
All rights reserved
ISBN 978-1-4413-0407-0
Printed in China

7 6 5 4 3 2

Visit us at www.peterpauper.com